The Art of Nailing Any Interview

It's time to step into the interview room with confidence.

The Art of Nailing Any Interview

© **Copyright 2021 - All rights reserved.**

The content contained within this book may not be reproduced, duplicated, or transmitted without direct written permission from the author or the publisher.

Under no circumstances will any blame or legal responsibility be held against the publisher, or author, for any damages, reparation, or monetary loss due to the information contained within this book. Either directly or indirectly. You are responsible for your own choices, actions, and results.

Legal Notice:

This book is copyright protected. This book is only for personal use. You cannot amend, distribute, sell, use, quote, or paraphrase any part, or the content within this book, without the consent of the author or publisher.

Disclaimer Notice:

Please note the information contained within this document is for educational and entertainment purposes only. All effort has been executed to present accurate-to-date, reliable, complete information. No warranties of any kind are declared or implied. Readers acknowledge that the author is not engaging in the rendering of legal, financial, medical, or professional advice. The content within this book has been derived from various sources. Please consult a licensed professional before attempting any techniques outlined in this book.

By reading this document, the reader agrees that under no circumstances is the author responsible for any losses, direct or indirect, which are incurred as a result of the use of the information contained within this document, including, but not limited to, — errors, omissions, or inaccuracies

Table of Contents

Introduction 8

The Power of Preparation 9

Understanding the Interview Process 13

Crafting Your Personal Brand 17

Researching the Company and Position 22

Analyzing the Job Description 27

Unveiling the Hidden Job Market 32

Polishing Your Resume and Cover Letter 38

Creating an Impressive Portfolio 43

Networking and Building Professional Relationships 48

Developing a Winning Mindset 53

Mastering Common Interview Questions 58

Nailing Behavioral and Situational Questions 63

Handling Challenging Interview Scenarios 68

Showcasing Your Skills and Experience 73

Demonstrating Cultural Fit and Teamwork 78

Making a Lasting Impression with Body Language 83

Handling Salary Negotiations and Benefits Discussions 88

Following Up After the Interview 93

Overcoming Rejection and Learning from Setbacks 98

Acing Virtual and Remote Interviews 103

Special Tips for Technical and Industry-Specific Interviews 108

Ethical and Professional Conduct in Interviews 113

Excelling in Panel and Group Interviews 118

Preparing for Second and Final Rounds 123

Resources for Continuous Interview Improvement 128

Conclusion: Launching Your Career with Confidence 133

Summary 138

Final Message 144

Introduction

These chapters cover various aspects of interview preparation, starting from understanding the interview process to post-interview follow-up.

They encompass topics such as personal branding, researching the company, crafting application materials, networking, answering different types of interview questions, handling challenging situations, showcasing skills and cultural fit, body language, salary negotiations, virtual interviews, industry-specific tips, ethical conduct, panel and group interviews, final rounds, and continuous improvement.

The conclusion chapter ties everything together, empowering readers to embark on their career journeys with confidence.

The Power of Preparation

In the competitive world of job hunting, it's essential to recognize the significant role that preparation plays in securing your dream job.

The power of preparation cannot be overstated. It sets the foundation for a successful interview experience and greatly increases your chances of standing out among other candidates.

In this chapter, we will explore why preparation is crucial, the benefits it offers, and how it can empower you to navigate the interview process with confidence.

The Purpose of Preparation

To embark on a journey toward interview success, it's important to understand the purpose of preparation. Preparation is not just about memorizing answers or rehearsing responses; it's about equipping yourself with the tools and knowledge necessary to present your best self to potential employers.

By investing time and effort in preparation, you demonstrate your commitment, dedication, and genuine interest in the position, which can significantly influence the interviewer's perception of you as a candidate.

Gaining a Competitive Edge

In today's competitive job market, standing out from the crowd is essential. Preparation gives you a competitive edge by enabling you to differentiate yourself from other candidates. It allows you to articulate your skills, experiences, and qualifications effectively, showcasing your unique value proposition.

Through thorough research and practice, you can align your strengths with the employer's needs, making a compelling case for why you are the ideal fit for the position.

Building Confidence

Preparation is the key to building confidence. When you have a deep understanding of the role, company, and interview process, you'll feel more self-assured and capable of handling any situation that arises.

Through meticulous preparation, you can anticipate and address potential challenges, giving you a sense of control and reducing anxiety. Confidence exudes professionalism and competence, leaving a lasting impression on interviewers.

Enhancing Interview Performance

Preparation directly impacts your interview performance. It allows you to familiarize yourself with common interview questions, enabling you to craft thoughtful and concise responses. By practicing your answers, you can refine your delivery, ensuring clarity and coherence.

Moreover, preparation equips you with examples and anecdotes that demonstrate your skills and experiences effectively. The more prepared you are, the more effortlessly you can navigate through different interview scenarios.

Tailoring Your Approach

Each job interview is unique, and preparation helps you tailor your approach accordingly. By researching the company, its values, and its mission, you gain valuable insights into its culture and expectations. This knowledge allows you to align your responses and showcase your fit within the organization.

Preparation also helps you anticipate specific interview formats, such as behavioral or situational questions, enabling you to provide targeted and compelling answers.

Overcoming Nervousness

Nervousness is a common experience during job interviews, but preparation acts as an antidote. When you are well-prepared, you can focus on showcasing your skills and qualifications rather than worrying about what might go wrong.

Preparation instills a sense of preparedness and readiness, minimizing nervousness and allowing you to project confidence and competence.

Conclusion

The power of preparation cannot be underestimated. It is the foundation upon which interview success is built. By investing time and effort into preparing for your job interviews, you gain a competitive edge, build confidence, enhance your interview performance, tailor your approach, and overcome nervousness.

In the following chapters, we will delve deeper into the various aspects of interview preparation, equipping you with the knowledge and strategies to excel in any interview situation. Remember, success favors the prepared mind.

Understanding the Interview Process

To navigate the job interview process successfully, it's crucial to have a comprehensive understanding of its various stages and components. In this chapter, we will explore the interview process from start to finish, shedding light on its purpose, typical stages, and the expectations of both candidates and employers.

By gaining insights into the interview process, you'll be better equipped to prepare effectively and confidently engage with potential employers.

The Purpose of the Interview Process

The interview process serves as a means for employers to assess the suitability of candidates for a specific role. It allows them to evaluate a candidate's qualifications, skills, experience, cultural fit, and potential contributions to the organization.

For candidates, the interview process presents an opportunity to showcase their abilities, convey their enthusiasm, and gather information about the company and position.

Pre-Interview Steps

Before the actual interview, there are several essential pre-interview steps. These include submitting an application (resume and cover letter), researching the company, and tailoring your application materials to highlight your relevant skills and experiences.

Employers often use these materials to shortlist candidates for further evaluation.

Screening and Initial Contact

After the initial application review, employers may conduct a screening process to narrow down the candidate pool. This may involve phone screenings or online assessments to evaluate basic qualifications, communication skills, and interest in the position.

If you pass this stage, you'll typically receive an invitation for an in-person or virtual interview.

Types of Interviews

Interviews can take various formats, depending on the employer's preferences and the nature of the role. Common types of interviews include traditional one-on-one interviews, panel interviews with multiple interviewers, group interviews with other candidates, technical interviews to assess specific skills, and behavioral interviews to gauge past experiences and problem-solving abilities.

Understanding the different interview formats will help you prepare accordingly and adapt your approach.

Interview Structure and Components

Interviews generally consist of multiple components designed to assess different aspects of a candidate's suitability. These components may include introductions and icebreakers, questions about your background and experience, behavioral or situational questions, technical assessments, case studies, role plays, and opportunities for candidates to ask their own questions.

Being familiar with these components allows you to anticipate what to expect and prepare accordingly.

Evaluation Criteria

Employers typically have specific evaluation criteria that guide their decision-making process. These criteria may include technical proficiency, communication skills, problem-solving abilities, cultural fit, leadership potential, adaptability, and teamwork.

By understanding these evaluation criteria, you can tailor your responses and provide examples that align with what employers are seeking.

Post-Interview Steps

Once the interview is concluded, there are post-interview steps to consider. These may include sending a thank-you note or email to express gratitude and reiterate your interest, following up on the status of the hiring process, and continuing to engage with the company in a professional manner until a final decision is reached.

Conclusion

Understanding the interview process is essential for successful navigation. By comprehending the purpose of the interview process, knowing the various stages, recognizing the different types of interviews, understanding the components, and being aware of the evaluation criteria, you can approach each interview with confidence and clarity.

In the next chapters, we will delve deeper into specific aspects of interview preparation to ensure you're well-equipped to excel at each stage of the process.

Crafting Your Personal Brand

In today's competitive job market, it's not enough to have the necessary qualifications and skills.

To stand out among other candidates, you must develop a strong personal brand that showcases your unique value proposition.

In this chapter, we will explore the concept of personal branding, its importance in the job search process, and practical steps you can take to craft a compelling and authentic personal brand.

Understanding Personal Branding

Your personal brand is the unique combination of your skills, experiences, values, and personality that sets you apart from others. It is how you present yourself to potential employers and colleagues, both online and offline.

Personal branding involves defining and communicating your distinct identity and the value you bring to the table. It helps establish a positive and memorable impression, making you more appealing to employers.

Your Strengths and Differentiators

To craft an effective personal brand, you must start by identifying your strengths and differentiators. Reflect on your skills, experiences, and unique qualities that make you stand out. Consider your expertise, accomplishments, and areas where you excel.

Identify the qualities or attributes that differentiate you from other candidates. This self-assessment will form the foundation of your personal brand.

Defining Your Brand Identity

Once you have identified your strengths and differentiators, it's time to define your brand identity. Start by clarifying your professional goals, values, and passions.

Determine what you want to be known for and the impression you want to leave on others. Craft a clear and concise personal brand statement that communicates your unique selling proposition and captures the essence of who you are as a professional.

Developing Consistent Brand Messaging

Consistency is key when it comes to personal branding.

Ensure that your brand messaging is consistent across all channels and touchpoints. This includes your resume, cover letter, social media profiles, networking interactions, and interviews.

Develop a compelling elevator pitch that effectively communicates your personal brand within a concise timeframe. Consistency in your messaging reinforces your brand identity and enhances your professional image.

Optimizing Your Online Presence

In today's digital age, your online presence plays a vital role in shaping your personal brand. Review and update your social media profiles, ensuring they align with your brand identity.

Utilize platforms like LinkedIn to showcase your expertise, connect with industry professionals, and share valuable content.

Create a professional website or portfolio to highlight your achievements and showcase your work. Optimizing your online presence enhances your credibility and visibility to potential employers.

Cultivating a Professional Image

Your personal brand extends beyond your skills and qualifications. It encompasses your professional image as well. Pay attention to your appearance, dress professionally for interviews, and maintain a positive and confident demeanor.

Develop strong communication and interpersonal skills to effectively convey your personal brand in various professional settings. Act with integrity and professionalism, both online and offline, to strengthen your brand reputation.

Building a Strong Network

Networking plays a crucial role in personal branding. Connect with professionals in your industry, attend industry events, and engage in meaningful conversations.

Nurture relationships with mentors, colleagues, and industry influencers who can help amplify your personal brand.

Collaborate on projects, contribute to discussions, and share your expertise to establish yourself as a trusted authority in your field.

Evolving Your Brand

As you grow and develop professionally, your personal brand may evolve. Continuously reassess and refine your personal brand to stay relevant and aligned with your career goals.

Seek feedback from mentors and trusted colleagues to gain insights into how others perceive your brand and make necessary adjustments. Embrace new challenges and opportunities that align with your personal brand, allowing it to evolve organically.

Conclusion

Crafting a compelling personal brand is a powerful tool in your job search arsenal. By identifying your strengths, defining your brand identity, developing consistent messaging, optimizing your online presence, cultivating a professional image, building a strong network, and evolving your brand over time, you can create a strong and authentic personal brand that resonates with potential employers.

In the next chapters, we will delve into specific strategies for researching companies, tailoring your application materials, and effectively showcasing your personal brand during the interview process.

Researching the Company and Position

Effective research is a fundamental step in preparing for a job interview.

By thoroughly understanding the company and the position you are applying for, you can demonstrate your knowledge, alignment with the organization's values, and your genuine interest in the role.

In this chapter, we will explore the importance of researching the company and position, as well as practical strategies to gather information that will empower you during the interview process.

Why Research Matters

Researching the company and position is essential for several reasons. It allows you to tailor your application materials and interview responses to align with the company's values, culture, and specific needs. It helps you demonstrate your genuine interest in the role, as well as your enthusiasm for contributing to the organization's success.

Research also equips you with valuable insights that can be leveraged to ask thoughtful questions during the interview, further showcasing your preparedness and engagement.

Understanding the Company

Start your research by gaining a deep understanding of the company you are applying to. Explore its mission statement, vision, and values. Familiarize yourself with its products, services, and target market. Learn about the company's history, its achievements, and any recent news or developments.

Investigate its organizational structure, key stakeholders, and competitors. This knowledge will provide a solid foundation for crafting tailored application materials and engaging in meaningful conversations during the interview.

Exploring the Company Culture

Understanding the company culture is crucial in assessing your fit within the organization. Research employee testimonials, company reviews, and any available information about the company's work environment. Look for indicators of the company's values, employee satisfaction, and the level of collaboration and innovation.

Consider how your own work style and preferences align with the company culture and be prepared to discuss how you can contribute positively to the team dynamic.

Analyzing the Position

In addition to researching the company, it's important to delve into the specific position you are applying for. Carefully review the job description, paying attention to the required qualifications, responsibilities, and desired skills. Identify the key challenges and objectives associated with the role.

Research industry trends and best practices related to the position and consider how your own experiences and expertise align with those requirements.

This knowledge will enable you to tailor your application materials and showcase your fit during the interview.

Leveraging Online Resources

The internet provides a wealth of resources for researching companies and positions. Explore the company's official website, paying attention to their About Us section, press releases, and blog posts. Follow the company's social media accounts to stay updated on recent news and announcements.

LinkedIn can be particularly valuable for researching the company, exploring employee profiles, and gaining insights into the company's culture and values. Additionally, industry-specific forums and websites can provide further insights and perspectives.

Tapping into Your Network

Your professional network can be an excellent resource for gathering information about the company and position. Reach out to current or former employees, industry peers, or individuals with knowledge of the company.

Request informational interviews or informal conversations to gain insights into the company's culture, work environment, and any specific details that may be helpful during the interview process. Networking connections can provide valuable firsthand perspectives and insider knowledge.

Taking Notes and Organizing Information

As you conduct your research, it's important to take organized notes to ensure you can easily reference the information later. Create a system for organizing key details, such as company values, notable achievements, and specific aspects of the job description.

This will help you recall important information during the interview and craft tailored responses that demonstrate your understanding of the company and position.

Conclusion:

Thoroughly researching the company and position is a crucial step in interview preparation.

By understanding the company's mission, values, products, and culture, as well as analyzing the position's requirements and objectives, you can demonstrate your knowledge, alignment, and genuine interest. Utilize online resources, tap into your network, and organize your findings to ensure you have the necessary information at your fingertips.

In the next chapters, we will explore strategies for tailoring your application materials and effectively showcasing your research during the interview process.

Analyzing the Job Description

The job description serves as a roadmap for both employers and candidates throughout the hiring process.

By carefully analyzing the job description, you can gain valuable insights into the position's requirements, responsibilities, and desired qualifications.

This chapter will guide you through the process of effectively analyzing a job description to understand its key components and tailor your application materials and interview responses accordingly.

Understanding the Purpose of the Job Description

The job description outlines the essential details of the position, including its purpose, responsibilities, required qualifications, and expectations. It serves as a communication tool between the employer and potential candidates, ensuring alignment and clarity throughout the hiring process.

By thoroughly analyzing the job description, you can demonstrate your understanding of the role and highlight your relevant skills and experiences.

Identifying Key Responsibilities

Start by identifying the key responsibilities outlined in the job description. Pay attention to the specific tasks, projects, and deliverables mentioned. Take note of the core functions of the role and consider how your own skills and experiences align with these responsibilities.

This analysis will enable you to showcase your relevant qualifications and demonstrate your ability to excel in the position.

Assessing Required Qualifications

Next, carefully review the required qualifications listed in the job description. These may include educational background, years of experience, technical skills, certifications, and specific competencies.

Assess your own qualifications in relation to these requirements. Identify areas where you meet or exceed the expectations and highlight those in your application materials and interview responses. For any gaps, consider how you can address them or emphasize transferable skills that demonstrate your ability to adapt and learn.

Identifying Desired Qualifications

In addition to required qualifications, job descriptions often include desired qualifications that may not be mandatory but are preferred by the employer.

These may include specific industry experience, advanced technical skills, leadership abilities, or language proficiency. Take note of the desired qualifications and assess your own background to determine if you possess any of these qualities.

Highlight any relevant experiences or skills that align with the desired qualifications, showcasing your added value as a candidate.

Understanding the Company's Expectations

Job descriptions often provide insights into the company's expectations for the position. This may include performance indicators, metrics, or goals that the candidate is expected to achieve.

Analyze these expectations and consider how your skills, experiences, and achievements align with them. Identify examples from your past experiences that demonstrate your ability to meet or exceed these expectations and be prepared to discuss them during the interview.

Noting Additional Details

While the core responsibilities and qualifications are crucial, job descriptions may also include additional details that provide context or highlight specific aspects of the role.

These details may include information about the team structure, reporting lines, company culture, benefits, or opportunities for growth.

Take note of these additional details as they can help you tailor your application materials and interview responses to demonstrate your fit with the organization and your long-term career goals.

Researching Beyond the Job Description

While the job description provides a foundation, it's essential to research beyond its contents.

Explore the company's website, social media presence, and industry-related sources to gather additional information about the company's culture, values, recent projects, or initiatives.

This broader understanding will enable you to craft more targeted application materials and engage in meaningful conversations during the interview.

Conclusion

Analyzing the job description is a crucial step in preparing for a job interview.

By understanding the key responsibilities, required and desired qualifications, and the company's expectations, you can tailor your application materials and interview responses to demonstrate your alignment with the position.

The next chapters will delve into strategies for effectively showcasing your qualifications and experiences to stand out as the ideal candidate for the role.

Unveiling the Hidden Job Market

While many job opportunities are advertised through traditional channels, a significant portion of the job market remains hidden or unadvertised.

These hidden job opportunities can provide unique advantages for job seekers, including reduced competition and access to exclusive positions.

In this chapter, we will explore strategies for uncovering the hidden job market, tapping into hidden job opportunities, and maximizing your chances of securing employment.

Understanding the Hidden Job Market

The hidden job market refers to job openings that are not publicly advertised or easily accessible through conventional job boards or recruitment platforms.

These positions are often filled through internal referrals, networking, or direct approaches from candidates who have proactively connected with the company.

Understanding the existence and dynamics of the hidden job market is essential for expanding your job search prospects.

Building a Strong Professional Network

Networking is a powerful tool for accessing the hidden job market. Cultivate and expand your professional network by attending industry events, joining relevant associations, and engaging in online communities.

Actively connect with professionals in your field and maintain relationships with colleagues, mentors, and industry influencers.

By nurturing your network, you increase your chances of being informed about hidden job opportunities and receiving referrals from trusted contacts.

Conducting Informational Interviews

Informational interviews are a valuable strategy for uncovering hidden job opportunities.

Reach out to professionals in your desired industry or companies of interest and request informational interviews to learn more about their experiences, insights, and potential job openings.

These conversations allow you to establish relationships, demonstrate your enthusiasm and knowledge, and gain insider information about unadvertised positions. Leverage these opportunities to expand your network and uncover hidden job leads.

Utilizing Online Professional Platforms

Online professional platforms, such as LinkedIn, offer opportunities to tap into the hidden job market. Optimize your LinkedIn profile to showcase your skills, experiences, and career interests.

Actively engage with industry professionals and companies by participating in discussions, sharing valuable content, and reaching out to individuals who may have insights into unadvertised job openings.

Networking on these platforms can open doors to hidden job opportunities and foster connections with decision-makers.

Recruitment Agencies and Headhunters

Recruitment agencies and headhunters have access to exclusive job opportunities that may not be publicly advertised.

Research and connect with reputable agencies in your industry or desired field. Share your career goals, skills, and experiences with them, and inquire about any hidden job openings they may have in their pipeline.

Building relationships with recruitment professionals can provide you with valuable insights and increase your visibility in the hidden job market.

Exploring Direct Company Approaches

Taking a proactive approach by directly contacting companies of interest can uncover hidden job opportunities. Research organizations that align with your career goals and values.

Visit their websites, look for potential job openings, and identify key decision-makers or department heads. Craft a compelling cover letter or email expressing your interest in working for the company and highlighting your qualifications.

By directly approaching companies, you demonstrate initiative and increase your chances of being considered for unadvertised positions.

Tapping into Professional Associations and Industry Events

Professional associations and industry events are rich sources of hidden job opportunities. Join relevant associations in your field and actively participate in their events, conferences, and networking sessions.

These platforms provide access to industry-specific job boards, insider information, and connections with professionals who may have knowledge of unadvertised positions.

Engaging in such activities expands your reach and increases your visibility within the hidden job market.

Staying Informed and Adapting

The hidden job market is dynamic, and job opportunities can arise unexpectedly. Stay informed about industry trends, company expansions, and changes within your field.

Set up job alerts on various platforms and regularly check company websites for updates. Remain adaptable and open to exploring different avenues, as hidden job opportunities may present themselves when you least expect them.

Conclusion

Unveiling the hidden job market requires proactive networking, strategic approaches, and a willingness to tap into unadvertised opportunities.

By building a strong professional network, conducting informational interviews, utilizing online platforms, connecting with recruitment agencies, and exploring direct approaches, you can maximize your chances of accessing hidden job opportunities.

Embrace the dynamic nature of the hidden job market, stay informed, and adapt your job search strategies accordingly.

The next chapters will focus on preparing for interviews and showcasing your skills and qualifications effectively to secure your desired job.

Polishing Your Resume and Cover Letter

Your resume and cover letter are essential tools for making a positive first impression on potential employers.

They serve as your marketing materials, highlighting your skills, experiences, and qualifications.

In this chapter, we will explore strategies for polishing your resume and cover letter to effectively showcase your professional background and increase your chances of landing an interview.

Understanding the Purpose of a Resume

A resume is a concise document that summarizes your relevant professional background, education, skills, and accomplishments.

Its purpose is to provide a snapshot of your qualifications and entice employers to learn more about you.

Understand the specific requirements of the position and tailor your resume accordingly, focusing on the most relevant information that demonstrates your fit for the role.

Structuring Your Resume

Create a clear and organized structure for your resume.

Begin with a compelling summary or objective statement that highlights your career goals and key qualifications.

Follow this with sections such as education, work experience, skills, certifications, and additional relevant information.

Use bullet points and concise phrases to convey information effectively. Prioritize the most relevant and impactful details and use reverse chronological order for work experience.

Showcasing Achievements and Impact

Incorporate specific achievements and the impact you made in your previous roles.

Quantify your accomplishments wherever possible, using metrics and numbers to demonstrate your contributions.

Focus on results, such as revenue growth, cost savings, project successes, or recognition received.

By showcasing your achievements, you provide concrete evidence of your capabilities and differentiate yourself from other candidates.

Tailoring Your Resume to the Job

Customize your resume for each job application by aligning it with the specific requirements of the position.

Analyze the job description and identify keywords, skills, and qualifications sought by the employer. Incorporate these keywords into your resume, especially in the skills and summary sections.

Highlight experiences and achievements that directly relate to the job, demonstrating your suitability for the role.

Crafting an Effective Cover Letter

A cover letter is an opportunity to personalize your application and express your motivation for the position.

Address the hiring manager by name if possible and introduce yourself with a compelling opening paragraph.

Clearly state your interest in the role and demonstrate your knowledge of the company.

Highlight key qualifications, experiences, and achievements that make you a strong candidate.

Use the cover letter to tell a story about your professional journey and explain how your skills align with the company's needs.

Showcasing Transferable Skills

Emphasize transferable skills that are relevant to the position, even if they were acquired in a different industry or role.

Analyze the job requirements and identify skills that are applicable across different contexts.

Highlight these transferable skills in both your resume and cover letter, demonstrating your adaptability and the value you can bring to the organization.

Ensuring Readability and Visual Appeal

Make sure your resume is visually appealing and easy to read. Use a clean and professional font and ensure appropriate font sizes and spacing. Organize information using headings, subheadings, and bullet points for clarity. Avoid large blocks of text and utilize white space effectively.

Proofread your resume and cover letter thoroughly to eliminate any grammatical or spelling errors.

Seeking Feedback and Proofreading

Seek feedback from trusted individuals, such as mentors or career advisors, to get an outside perspective on your resume and cover letter. They can provide valuable insights, identify areas of improvement, and ensure your documents effectively communicate your qualifications.

Additionally, proofread your materials carefully to eliminate any typos or inconsistencies.

Conclusion

Polishing your resume and cover letter is crucial for making a strong impression on potential employers. Tailor your documents to the specific job requirements, highlight achievements and transferable skills, and ensure readability and visual appeal. Seek feedback and proofread meticulously to present yourself as a qualified and professional candidate.

The next chapters will focus on interview preparation and strategies for confidently showcasing your qualifications.

Creating an Impressive Portfolio

In addition to your resume and cover letter, a portfolio is a powerful tool for showcasing your skills, accomplishments, and creativity to potential employers.

It provides tangible evidence of your abilities and allows you to present your work in a visually appealing and organized manner.

This chapter will guide you through the process of creating an impressive portfolio that effectively highlights your professional achievements.

Defining Your Portfolio's Purpose

Before creating your portfolio, determine its purpose. Are you showcasing design projects, writing samples, coding projects, or a combination of different works?

Understanding the purpose will help you structure and curate your portfolio accordingly. Consider the industry and the type of job you're applying for to ensure that your portfolio aligns with the desired expectations and requirements.

Selecting the Right Samples

Carefully select the samples you include in your portfolio. Choose works that are relevant to the job you're seeking and demonstrate your skills and expertise.

Show diversity in your portfolio by including a range of projects that highlight different aspects of your abilities. If possible, select samples that have had a positive impact or received recognition. Quality is more important than quantity, so focus on showcasing your best work.

Organizing and Structuring Your Portfolio

Create a logical and user-friendly structure for your portfolio. Consider categorizing your samples based on projects, industries, or specific skills.

Provide clear titles and descriptions for each sample, explaining the context, your role, and the objectives of the project. Use a consistent layout and design throughout your portfolio to maintain a cohesive visual identity.

Utilizing Digital Platforms

In today's digital age, creating an online portfolio is highly recommended. Use platforms such as Behance, Dribbble, GitHub, or personal websites to showcase your work.

These platforms offer customization options and allow you to present your samples in an engaging and interactive way. Additionally, make sure your portfolio is accessible on multiple devices, including desktop and mobile, to cater to a wider audience.

Showcasing Process and Problem-Solving Skills

In addition to final results, include samples that demonstrate your process and problem-solving abilities. This could include sketches, wireframes, prototypes, or documentation.

By showcasing your thought process, you provide insight into your problem-solving approach and the value you bring to the table. Explain your methodology and the steps you took to achieve the end result.

Highlighting Collaborative Projects

If you have collaborated on projects, include them in your portfolio. Highlight your role within the team, the collaborative process, and the outcome achieved.

This demonstrates your ability to work effectively in a team setting and showcases your interpersonal skills. Provide details on how you contributed to the project and the impact of your collaboration.

Incorporating Testimonials and Recommendations

To add credibility to your portfolio, include testimonials or recommendations from clients, colleagues, or supervisors.

These endorsements validate your skills and provide third-party perspectives on your work. Select testimonials that specifically address your strengths and highlight your contributions to the projects mentioned in your portfolio. Ensure you have permission to use the testimonials and attribute them to the respective individuals.

Keeping Your Portfolio Updated

Regularly update your portfolio to reflect your latest work and accomplishments. Remove outdated or less relevant samples and replace them with new, more compelling ones.

Keep your portfolio fresh and reflective of your current skills and interests. This demonstrates your commitment to growth and showcases your ability to stay up-to-date in your field.

Seeking Feedback and Testing

Before sharing your portfolio with potential employers, seek feedback from trusted peers, mentors, or industry professionals. They can provide valuable insights on the content, layout, and overall impact of your portfolio. Test your portfolio on different devices and browsers to ensure it displays correctly and functions seamlessly.

Address any feedback or issues identified to present the best possible version of your portfolio.

Conclusion

Creating an impressive portfolio is essential for showcasing your skills, abilities, and accomplishments to potential employers.

By selecting the right samples, organizing your portfolio effectively, utilizing digital platforms, highlighting process and collaboration, incorporating testimonials, and keeping it updated, you can present a compelling narrative of your professional journey.

Your portfolio serves as a visual representation of your expertise and creativity, enhancing your chances of standing out in a competitive job market.

Networking and Building Professional Relationships

Networking and building professional relationships are crucial aspects of a successful job search and career development.

Building a strong network can provide access to job opportunities, industry insights, mentorship, and valuable connections.

In this chapter, we will explore strategies for effective networking, cultivating professional relationships, and leveraging them to advance your career.

Understanding the Power of Networking

Networking involves establishing and nurturing relationships with professionals in your field or industry. It expands your reach, exposes you to new opportunities, and provides a support system for career growth.

Recognize that networking is not just about immediate benefits but also about building long-term connections that can lead to future opportunities.

Developing a Networking Strategy

Create a networking strategy to guide your efforts. Determine your goals, such as finding mentors, exploring job opportunities, or expanding your knowledge. Identify target industries, companies, and individuals who align with your career aspirations.

Set specific networking objectives, such as attending industry events, joining professional associations, or connecting with individuals on LinkedIn.

Attending Industry Events and Conferences

Industry events and conferences provide excellent networking opportunities. Attend relevant conferences, trade shows, seminars, and workshops.

Engage in conversations with fellow attendees, speakers, and exhibitors. Ask thoughtful questions, share your insights, and exchange contact information.

Follow up with the connections you make after the event to nurture relationships further.

Joining Professional Associations and Groups

Professional associations and groups offer a platform to connect with like-minded individuals in your industry. Research and join associations related to your field.

Engage actively by attending meetings, participating in forums, and volunteering for committees. Networking within these associations allows you to connect with experienced professionals, gain industry insights, and access exclusive job opportunities.

Utilizing Online Networking Platforms

Online networking platforms, such as LinkedIn, offer immense opportunities for connecting with professionals worldwide. Optimize your LinkedIn profile, highlighting your skills, experiences, and career goals.

Actively engage by sharing valuable content, participating in discussions, and connecting with industry leaders. Personalize connection requests to establish meaningful relationships and nurture connections over time.

Leveraging Informational Interviews

Informational interviews are not only useful for job exploration but also for building relationships. Request informational interviews with professionals in your field to learn from their experiences and insights.

Prepare thoughtful questions, actively listen, and express gratitude for their time. These conversations can lead to mentorship, referrals, or future collaborations.

Building and Maintaining Relationships

Networking is not just about making initial connections but also about cultivating and maintaining relationships.

Follow up with individuals you meet, expressing appreciation for their time and insights. Keep in touch regularly by sharing relevant articles, congratulating them on their achievements, or offering assistance when needed.

Genuine relationships are built on mutual support and reciprocity.

Offering Value to Others

Networking is a two-way street. Look for opportunities to offer value to your connections. Share industry-related insights, recommend useful resources, or make introductions when appropriate.

Actively support and promote the work of your connections. By being a valuable resource and connector, you solidify your position within your network.

Nurturing Mentoring Relationships

Seek out mentors who can guide you in your career journey. Approach experienced professionals you admire and respectfully request their mentorship.

Be clear about your goals and expectations, and maintain regular communication. Show gratitude for their guidance and make the most of their insights and expertise.

Conclusion

Networking and building professional relationships are essential for career growth and success.

By developing a networking strategy, attending industry events, joining professional associations, utilizing online platforms, leveraging informational interviews, and nurturing relationships, you can expand your network, gain valuable insights, and access new opportunities.

Cultivating genuine connections and offering value to others creates a supportive and collaborative professional ecosystem that can propel your career forward.

Developing a Winning Mindset

A winning mindset is a powerful asset that can fuel your success in the job search process and beyond.

It is a mindset characterized by resilience, confidence, positivity, and a proactive approach to challenges.

In this chapter, we will explore strategies for developing a winning mindset to overcome obstacles, stay motivated, and achieve your career goals.

Embracing a Growth Mindset

Adopt a growth mindset, believing that your abilities and intelligence can be developed through dedication and effort.

Embrace challenges as opportunities for growth, view failures as learning experiences, and maintain a positive attitude towards continuous improvement. Cultivating a growth mindset allows you to embrace new opportunities and approach setbacks with resilience.

Setting Realistic and Ambitious Goals

Set clear, realistic, and ambitious goals for your career. Break them down into smaller, actionable steps that you can work towards. Setting specific, measurable, attainable, relevant, and time-bound (SMART) goals keeps you focused and motivated.

Regularly review and adjust your goals as needed to stay on track and maintain a sense of purpose.

Visualizing Success

Visualize your success and the outcomes you desire. Create mental images of achieving your goals, excelling in interviews, and securing your dream job.

Visualization helps align your thoughts and actions, boosts your confidence, and enhances your belief in your abilities.

Use visualization techniques regularly to reinforce your positive mindset and create a sense of self-assurance.

Practicing Positive Self-Talk

Monitor and consciously redirect negative self-talk toward positive and empowering thoughts. Replace self-doubt with self-belief and affirmations.

Remind yourself of your strengths, accomplishments, and the progress you've made.

Positive self-talk cultivates a confident and resilient mindset, enabling you to tackle challenges with optimism and perseverance.

Managing Stress and Resilience

Develop effective stress management techniques to maintain your mental and emotional well-being throughout the job search process. Practice self-care activities such as exercise, meditation, deep breathing, or engaging in hobbies.

Build resilience by reframing setbacks as temporary obstacles and learning opportunities. Seek support from friends, family, or a mentor during challenging times.

Embracing a Proactive Approach

Take control of your job search and career development by adopting a proactive approach.

Instead of waiting for opportunities to come to you, actively seek them out. Reach out to professionals in your field, attend networking events, and engage in informational interviews.

Proactivity demonstrates your commitment and determination, increasing your chances of finding the right opportunities.

Celebrating Achievements, Big and Small

Acknowledge and celebrate your achievements along the way, both big and small. Recognize the progress you've made, milestones reached, and goals accomplished.

Celebrating achievements boosts your confidence, reinforces your positive mindset, and provides motivation to keep moving forward.

Take time to appreciate your hard work and the steps you've taken toward your career goals.

Seeking Inspiration and Learning Opportunities

Surround yourself with sources of inspiration and continuous learning.

Read books, articles, and success stories related to your industry or field. Attend workshops, webinars, and conferences to stay updated on industry trends and expand your knowledge.

Engage in professional development activities to enhance your skills and broaden your perspectives.

Building a Supportive Network

Surround yourself with a supportive network of friends, mentors, and like-minded professionals who uplift and inspire you. Seek advice, guidance, and encouragement from your network during challenging times.

Collaborate with others, share experiences, and learn from their journeys. A strong support system provides motivation, accountability, and valuable insights.

Conclusion

Developing a winning mindset is a transformative journey that empowers you to navigate the job search process with confidence, resilience, and a proactive approach.

By embracing a growth mindset, setting goals, visualizing success, practicing positive self-talk, managing stress, being proactive, celebrating achievements, seeking inspiration, and building a supportive network, you can cultivate a mindset that propels you toward success in your career and beyond.

Remember, your mindset shapes your actions, and your actions shape your outcomes.

Mastering Common Interview Questions

Interviews often include a series of common questions designed to assess your qualifications, skills, and fit for the job.

Mastering these questions is essential to make a positive impression and increase your chances of success.

In this chapter, we will explore strategies for effectively answering common interview questions and showcasing your abilities with confidence.

Understanding the Purpose of Common Interview Questions

Common interview questions serve multiple purposes, such as assessing your qualifications, gauging your problem-solving skills, evaluating your cultural fit, and understanding your career aspirations.

Recognize that interviewers use these questions to gain insights into your experience, personality, and potential contributions to the organization.

Preparing Thoughtful Responses

Take the time to prepare thoughtful and well-structured responses to common interview questions. Reflect on your experiences, accomplishments, and challenges faced throughout your career.

Align your responses with the specific requirements and values of the company. Practice your answers to ensure clarity, conciseness, and coherence.

Showcasing Your Strengths and Accomplishments

Use common interview questions as an opportunity to highlight your strengths and accomplishments. Structure your responses to emphasize your relevant skills, experiences, and achievements.

Provide specific examples that demonstrate your abilities and the impact you made in previous roles. Quantify your achievements whenever possible to add credibility to your claims.

Demonstrating Problem-Solving and Critical Thinking Skills

Many interview questions assess your problem-solving and critical-thinking abilities. Be prepared to share how you have approached challenges, resolved conflicts, or made difficult decisions in the past.

Walk the interviewer through your thought process, explaining the steps you took to analyze the situation, consider alternatives, and arrive at a solution.

Addressing Behavioral and Situational Questions

Behavioral and situational questions require you to draw from your past experiences to predict your future actions.

Use the STAR method (Situation, Task, Action, Result) to structure your responses. Describe the specific situation or task, explain the actions you took, and highlight the positive results achieved. This format provides a clear and concise framework for addressing these types of questions.

Expressing Your Career Goals and Motivation

Interviewers often inquire about your career goals and motivation for applying to the position. Be prepared to articulate your short-term and long-term career objectives, highlighting how they align with the role and the company's mission.

Show enthusiasm for the opportunity and convey your genuine interest in contributing to the organization's success.

Addressing Weaknesses and Challenges

When asked about your weaknesses or challenges, approach the question with honesty and self-awareness. Focus on areas where you have actively sought growth and improvement.

Discuss how you have addressed these challenges and the steps you have taken to overcome them. Demonstrate a willingness to learn and develop professionally.

Adapting to Different Interview Formats

Interview formats can vary, including phone interviews, video interviews, panel interviews, or behavioral interviews.

Familiarize yourself with the specific format you will be encountering and prepare accordingly. Adjust your communication style, maintain eye contact (if applicable), and project confidence and professionalism in different interview settings.

Active Listening and Effective Communication

During interviews, practice active listening to ensure you understand the question fully before responding. Take your time to craft your answers thoughtfully. Use clear and concise language and avoid rambling or going off-topic.

Demonstrate effective communication skills by using appropriate body language, maintaining a confident tone, and being attentive to the interviewer's cues.

Conclusion

Mastering common interview questions is a key component of interview success.

By understanding the purpose of these questions, preparing thoughtful responses, showcasing your strengths and accomplishments, demonstrating problem-solving skills, expressing your career goals, addressing weaknesses, adapting to different interview formats, practicing active listening, and communicating effectively, you can confidently navigate interviews and leave a lasting positive impression on potential employers.

Remember, preparation and practice are key to mastering the art of answering interview questions.

Nailing Behavioral and Situational Questions

Behavioral and situational questions are commonly used in interviews to assess how you handle specific situations and to evaluate your problem-solving skills.

Mastering these types of questions is crucial for demonstrating your abilities and suitability for the job.

In this chapter, we will delve into strategies for effectively answering behavioral and situational questions to showcase your competence and make a memorable impression.

Understanding Behavioral and Situational Questions

Behavioral questions focus on your past experiences and actions, while situational questions present hypothetical scenarios to assess your problem-solving abilities. Both types of questions aim to understand your decision-making process, interpersonal skills, and how you handle challenges.

Recognize the underlying purpose of these questions to provide targeted and impactful responses.

Utilizing the STAR Method

The STAR method (Situation, Task, Action, Result) is a widely used framework for answering behavioral and situational questions. Begin by describing the situation or task you encountered, explain the specific actions you took to address it, and conclude with the positive results you achieved.

This structured approach ensures clarity and helps interviewers follow your thought process.

Selecting Relevant Examples

Before the interview, review your past experiences and select examples that demonstrate your skills, achievements, and problem-solving abilities.

Choose examples that closely align with the job requirements and showcase the qualities the employer seeks. Be specific in your selection and ensure the examples highlight your competence in handling similar situations.

Highlighting Key Skills and Competencies

When answering behavioral and situational questions, emphasize the key skills and competencies that are relevant to the position.

Whether it's leadership, teamwork, adaptability, or analytical thinking, explicitly mention these skills in your responses. Connect your experiences to the skills and competencies sought by the employer, illustrating your suitability for the role.

Providing Context and Details

When discussing your experiences, provide sufficient context and details to paint a clear picture for the interviewer.

Describe the background of the situation, the specific challenges faced, and the stakeholders involved. Include relevant details about your role, responsibilities, and the actions you took to address the situation.

This level of specificity adds depth to your responses.

Demonstrating Problem-Solving Skills

Behavioral and situational questions often assess your problem-solving skills. Walk the interviewer through your problem-solving process, explaining the steps you took to analyze the situation, identify potential solutions, and make informed decisions.

Emphasize your ability to think critically, consider multiple perspectives, and collaborate with others to reach effective solutions.

Showcasing Interpersonal and Communication Skills

Behavioral and situational questions provide an opportunity to demonstrate your interpersonal and communication skills. Discuss how you effectively communicated with team members, stakeholders, or clients during challenging situations.

Highlight your ability to listen actively, resolve conflicts, and build positive relationships to achieve common goals.

Addressing Challenges and Lessons Learned

When sharing your experiences, be transparent about any challenges or setbacks you encountered. Discuss how you approached and overcame these obstacles, demonstrating resilience and a growth mindset.

Additionally, reflect on the lessons learned from these experiences and how they have shaped your approach to similar situations.

Practicing with Mock Interviews

To refine your responses to behavioral and situational questions, engage in mock interviews with a friend, mentor, or career counselor.

Practice articulating your examples using the STAR method, receive feedback on your communication style, and fine-tune your answers for clarity and conciseness.

Mock interviews help build confidence and enhance your performance during the actual interview.

Conclusion

Nailing behavioral and situational questions requires thoughtful preparation and effective communication.

By understanding the purpose of these questions, utilizing the STAR method, selecting relevant examples, highlighting key skills and competencies, providing context and details, demonstrating problem-solving and interpersonal skills, addressing challenges, and practicing with mock interviews, you can confidently tackle these questions and impress interviewers with your ability to handle real-world situations.

Remember, practice and preparation are essential to master the art of nailing behavioral and situational questions.

Handling Challenging Interview Scenarios

Interviews can sometimes present challenging scenarios that test your ability to think on your feet and respond effectively.

These scenarios may include tough questions, unexpected situations, or even dealing with difficult interviewers.

In this chapter, we will explore strategies for handling challenging interview scenarios with poise, professionalism, and confidence.

Remaining Calm and Composed

Challenging scenarios in interviews can evoke stress or nervousness. It is crucial to remain calm and composed throughout the process.

Take a deep breath, maintain good posture, and remind yourself of your preparedness. Project a confident and composed demeanor, as this will help you think clearly and respond effectively.

Active Listening and Seeking Clarification

If faced with a challenging or ambiguous question, listen attentively to ensure you fully understand what is being asked. If necessary, seek clarification or ask for additional information to ensure you provide a relevant and accurate response.

Active listening demonstrates your attentiveness and shows your commitment to understanding the interviewer's intentions.

Pausing and Collecting Your Thoughts

In challenging scenarios where you need a moment to gather your thoughts, it is perfectly acceptable to pause briefly before responding.

Take a breath, process the question or situation, and organize your thoughts. Use this pause to formulate a coherent and thoughtful response.

It is better to take a moment to collect your thoughts than to provide a rushed or incomplete answer.

Responding with Honesty and Integrity

When faced with tough questions, respond honestly and authentically. Avoid fabricating or exaggerating information. If you don't know the answer, it is acceptable to admit it, but express your willingness to learn and find a solution.

Demonstrating integrity and honesty in your responses builds trust and credibility with the interviewer.

Turning Negative Situations into Positive Opportunities

If confronted with a negative question or comment, reframe it as an opportunity to showcase your resilience, problem-solving skills, or growth mindset. Stay positive, focus on constructive aspects, and use the opportunity to highlight how you have overcome challenges in the past.

Show your ability to learn from difficult situations and use them as stepping stones for personal and professional growth.

Managing Difficult Interviewers

Dealing with difficult interviewers can be challenging. Remain professional, respectful, and composed throughout the interaction.

Listen carefully to their questions or comments and respond thoughtfully. Stay focused on your qualifications, experiences, and the value you can bring to the organization. Remember that their behavior may not reflect the overall company culture or the attitudes of potential colleagues.

Demonstrating Adaptability and Flexibility

Challenging scenarios may require adaptability and flexibility. Employers value candidates who can adjust to changing circumstances and demonstrate a willingness to learn and grow.

Show your adaptability by providing examples of how you have successfully adapted to new environments, tackled unexpected challenges, or embraced change in previous roles.

Leveraging Your Emotional Intelligence

Emotional intelligence plays a crucial role in handling challenging interview scenarios. Be aware of your emotions and manage them effectively.

Maintain a positive and professional demeanor, even in difficult situations. Display empathy, active listening, and effective communication skills to navigate and address any conflicts or challenges that arise during the interview.

Reflecting on the Experience

After the interview, take time to reflect on the challenging scenarios you encountered. Evaluate your responses, identify areas for improvement, and consider how you would approach similar situations in the future.

Learning from these experiences enhances your interview skills and prepares you for future encounters.

Conclusion

Handling challenging interview scenarios requires composure, adaptability, and effective communication.

By remaining calm, actively listening, pausing to collect your thoughts, responding honestly and with integrity, reframing negative situations, managing difficult interviewers, demonstrating adaptability, leveraging emotional intelligence, and reflecting on the experience, you can navigate challenging scenarios with confidence and professionalism.

Remember, how you handle these situations can leave a lasting impression on the interviewer and set you apart from other candidates.

Showcasing Your Skills and Experience

Effectively showcasing your skills and experience during an interview is essential for demonstrating your qualifications and suitability for the job.

In this chapter, we will explore strategies to highlight your skills, expertise, and accomplishments, enabling you to stand out as a top candidate and leave a lasting impression on interviewers.

Understanding the Job Requirements

Before the interview, thoroughly review the job description and understand the key requirements of the role. Identify the skills, qualifications, and experiences that are most relevant to the position.

This understanding will help you tailor your responses to showcase your alignment with the job requirements.

Aligning Your Experiences with the Job

During the interview, strategically connect your past experiences and accomplishments with the job requirements.

Highlight specific projects, achievements, and responsibilities that demonstrate your expertise in areas directly related to the role. Show how your skills and experience make you a valuable asset to the organization.

Providing Concrete Examples

When discussing your skills and experience, use concrete examples to substantiate your claims. Provide specific instances where you successfully applied your skills, overcame challenges, or achieved notable results.

Quantify your achievements whenever possible, using metrics or percentages to demonstrate the impact of your work.

Showcasing Transferable Skills

Even if you lack direct experience in certain areas, emphasize your transferable skills. Identify skills from your previous roles that apply to the position you are interviewing for.

Explain how these skills can be leveraged to contribute effectively to the new role. Showcase your ability to adapt and quickly learn new skills.

Demonstrating Leadership and Collaboration

Highlight your leadership and collaboration skills by sharing experiences where you successfully led teams, mentored colleagues, or fostered a positive work environment.

Discuss instances where you effectively collaborated with others to achieve shared goals and emphasize your ability to work well in a team-oriented environment.

Describing Problem-Solving Abilities

Demonstrate your problem-solving abilities by discussing challenges you faced in previous roles and the strategies you employed to overcome them.

Share examples where you analyzed complex problems, developed innovative solutions, and implemented effective strategies.

Showcase your critical thinking, analytical skills, and ability to make sound decisions.

Communicating Clear and Concise

When discussing your skills and experience, communicate your thoughts clearly and concisely. Avoid using technical jargon or overwhelming the interviewer with excessive details.

Focus on the most relevant aspects of your experience and use language that is easily understandable to non-technical or non-specialized individuals.

Highlighting Professional Development

Showcase your commitment to professional growth by discussing relevant courses, certifications, or workshops you have completed.

Highlight any additional training or educational experiences that have enhanced your skills and knowledge in the field.

This demonstrates your dedication to continuous improvement and staying updated in your industry.

Sharing Success Stories

Share success stories that highlight your achievements and the positive impact you have made in previous roles.

Frame these stories in the form of a narrative, providing context, outlining the challenges faced, explaining the actions taken, and highlighting the outcomes achieved.

These stories not only showcase your skills but also make you more memorable to the interviewer.

Conclusion

Effectively showcasing your skills and experience is a crucial aspect of a successful interview.

By aligning your experiences with the job requirements, providing concrete examples, demonstrating leadership and collaboration, describing problem-solving abilities, communicating clearly and concisely, highlighting professional development, and sharing success stories, you can impress interviewers and position yourself as the ideal candidate for the role.

Remember, confidence and authenticity are key to effectively showcasing your abilities and leaving a lasting impression.

Demonstrating Cultural Fit and Teamwork

In addition to assessing your skills and qualifications, employers often prioritize cultural fit and teamwork when evaluating candidates.

Demonstrating that you will thrive within their organizational culture and contribute effectively to a team is crucial.

In this chapter, we will explore strategies to showcase your cultural fit and teamwork abilities during the interview process.

Researching the Company Culture

Before the interview, thoroughly research the company's values, mission, and culture. Gain an understanding of the work environment, team dynamics, and any specific values or behaviors that the organization emphasizes.

This knowledge will enable you to align your responses and behaviors with the company's cultural expectations.

Highlighting Shared Values

During the interview, emphasize your alignment with the company's values and how they resonate with your own beliefs and work ethic.

Share examples that demonstrate your adherence to these values in previous roles, such as instances where you prioritized teamwork, integrity, innovation, or customer focus.

This showcases your ability to contribute to the company's culture positively.

Showcasing Adaptability

Highlight your adaptability and flexibility by discussing experiences where you successfully navigated diverse work environments or managed change effectively.

Demonstrate your openness to new ideas, willingness to collaborate with different personalities, and ability to thrive in dynamic situations.

This shows your capacity to integrate seamlessly into the existing team.

Sharing Collaborative Experiences

Emphasize your ability to work well within a team by sharing examples of successful collaborations.

Discuss projects where you collaborated with colleagues, stakeholders, or clients to achieve shared goals.

Highlight your active participation, effective communication, and the positive outcomes that resulted from your teamwork.

Demonstrating Effective Communication

Effective communication is vital for teamwork. Showcase your communication skills by providing examples of instances where you communicated clearly, listened actively, and fostered open dialogue within a team.

Discuss your ability to convey ideas, provide constructive feedback, and resolve conflicts in a professional and respectful manner.

Illustrating Emotional Intelligence

Employers value candidates who possess emotional intelligence and can navigate interpersonal relationships effectively.

Share examples where you demonstrated empathy, understanding, and adaptability in dealing with colleagues or clients.

Discuss situations where you actively supported team members, built strong working relationships, and fostered a positive work environment.

Describing Conflict Resolution

Teamwork often involves navigating conflicts or disagreements.

Demonstrate your ability to handle conflict by sharing examples of instances where you successfully resolved conflicts within a team.

Discuss your approach to identifying underlying issues, facilitating open discussions, and finding mutually beneficial resolutions.

Highlight your ability to maintain positive relationships even during challenging situations.

Displaying a Proactive Attitude

Employers seek candidates who take initiative and contribute actively to the team's success.

Share experiences where you took on additional responsibilities, proposed innovative ideas, or implemented process improvements that positively impacted the team or organization.

Highlight your proactive mindset and commitment to achieving collective goals.

Referencing Past Team Achievements

Highlight successful team achievements from your past experiences.

Discuss projects where you played a significant role in delivering exceptional results and emphasize the collaborative efforts that led to those accomplishments.

This demonstrates your ability to work effectively with others and contribute to a high-performing team.

Conclusion

Demonstrating cultural fit and teamwork abilities is essential to impress employers and secure a job offer.

By researching the company culture, highlighting shared values, showcasing adaptability, sharing collaborative experiences, demonstrating effective communication and emotional intelligence, describing conflict resolution skills, displaying a proactive attitude, and referencing past team achievements, you can effectively showcase your ability to integrate well within the organization and contribute to the team's success.

Remember, authenticity and genuine enthusiasm for teamwork are key to demonstrating your cultural fit and teamwork abilities.

Making a Lasting Impression with Body Language

Body language plays a significant role in how you are perceived during a job interview. Your nonverbal cues can convey confidence, professionalism, and engagement.

In this chapter, we will explore strategies to use body language effectively and make a lasting impression on interviewers.

Projecting Confidence

Confidence is essential during an interview. Stand tall, maintain good posture, and avoid slouching. Walk with purpose and enter the interview room with confidence.

Use a firm handshake while making eye contact with the interviewer. These actions project confidence and set a positive tone for the rest of the interview.

Active Listening

Engage in active listening to demonstrate your attentiveness and interest in the conversation.

Lean slightly forward to show your engagement and maintain eye contact with the interviewer. Nod occasionally to indicate understanding and use facial expressions to convey interest and empathy.

This nonverbal behavior showcases your active participation in the interview.

Smiling

A warm and genuine smile helps create a positive impression. Smile naturally throughout the interview, especially during introductions, positive interactions, and moments of agreement or enthusiasm.

However, avoid excessive or forced smiling, as it may appear insincere.

Gesturing Appropriately

Using appropriate hand gestures can enhance your communication and express enthusiasm.

Use natural and purposeful gestures to emphasize key points or demonstrate your understanding. However, be mindful of excessive or distracting gestures that can detract from your message.

Keep your movements controlled and in line with the context of the conversation.

Mirroring and Matching

Subtly mirroring or matching the interviewer's body language can establish rapport and a sense of connection. Pay attention to the interviewer's nonverbal cues and adopt similar postures, gestures, and facial expressions.

However, be cautious not to mimic or imitate them excessively, as it may come across as insincere or disrespectful.

Regulating Nervous Habits

Nervous habits such as tapping your foot, fidgeting with your hands, or playing with your hair can convey anxiety or lack of confidence.

Be aware of these habits and consciously work on reducing or eliminating them.

Practice deep breathing and engage in relaxation techniques before the interview to help manage nervousness.

Posture and Openness

Maintain an open and approachable posture by keeping your arms uncrossed and your body facing the interviewer.

This posture conveys openness, receptiveness, and confidence. Avoid crossing your arms or placing objects as barriers between you and the interviewer, as it can create a defensive or closed-off impression.

Vocal Tone and Volume

Body language extends beyond physical gestures. Pay attention to your vocal tone and volume as well. Speak clearly and confidently, using an appropriate volume that is audible without being too loud or too soft.

Vary your pitch and pace to add emphasis and maintain the interviewer's interest.

Managing Eye Contact

Maintaining appropriate eye contact is crucial for building trust and establishing a connection.

Look directly into the interviewer's eyes while speaking and listening. However, avoid staring excessively, as it can make the interviewer uncomfortable.

If there are multiple interviewers, distribute your eye contact evenly among them.

Conclusion

Your body language can greatly influence the impression you make during a job interview.

By projecting confidence, engaging in active listening, smiling genuinely, using appropriate gestures, mirroring and matching subtly, regulating nervous habits, maintaining an open posture, managing vocal tone and volume, and managing eye contact, you can make a lasting impression on interviewers.

Remember, practicing and being mindful of your body language enhances your overall communication and helps you convey professionalism, confidence, and interest in the opportunity.

Handling Salary Negotiations and Benefits Discussions

Navigating salary negotiations and benefits discussions can be a crucial aspect of the job interview process.

It is important to approach these conversations with preparation, confidence, and professionalism.

In this chapter, we will explore strategies to effectively handle salary negotiations and benefits discussions to ensure a mutually beneficial outcome.

Researching Market Value

Before entering into salary negotiations, conduct thorough research on the market value of the position you are applying for.

Explore salary ranges for similar roles in the industry, taking into account factors such as experience, location, and industry standards.

This knowledge will provide you with a baseline for negotiation and help you set realistic expectations.

Knowing Your Worth

Understand your own value and the unique contributions you bring to the table.

Reflect on your skills, qualifications, and experiences that make you stand out as a candidate. Identify any additional value you can bring to the organization, such as specialized certifications or unique expertise. This self-awareness will empower you during negotiations.

Deferring Salary Discussions

When possible, it is generally beneficial to defer salary discussions until you have a clear understanding of the job requirements and the organization's level of interest in hiring you.

Redirect the conversation towards your qualifications, fit for the role, and enthusiasm for the opportunity.

This allows you to build rapport and showcase your value before discussing compensation.

Highlighting Your Value Proposition

During salary negotiations, emphasize the value you bring to the organization.

Discuss your past accomplishments and the positive impact you have made in previous roles.

Demonstrate how your skills, expertise, and achievements align with the job requirements and contribute to the company's success.

This reinforces your value and justifies your desired compensation.

Expressing Flexibility

While it is important to have a clear idea of your salary expectations, expressing flexibility can be advantageous during negotiations.

Consider the entire compensation package, including benefits, bonuses, stock options, and opportunities for growth.

Communicate your willingness to discuss alternative forms of compensation to reach a mutually beneficial agreement.

Articulating Your Expectations

When discussing salary, be prepared to articulate your expectations clearly and confidently. State your desired salary range based on your research, taking into account your qualifications and the market value.

Be prepared to justify your expectations with concrete examples of your accomplishments, skills, and the value you bring to the organization.

Active Listening and Asking Questions

During benefits discussions, actively listen to the information provided by the interviewer or hiring manager.

Ask questions to gain a comprehensive understanding of the benefits package, including health insurance, retirement plans, vacation policies, and professional development opportunities.

This demonstrates your interest and thoroughness in evaluating the entire compensation package.

Negotiating with Professionalism

Approach negotiations with professionalism, respect, and a collaborative mindset. Keep the lines of communication open and engage in constructive dialogue.

Avoid becoming confrontational or making demands. Instead, focus on finding common ground and reaching a mutually beneficial agreement that satisfies both parties' needs.

Evaluating the Entire Package

When assessing a job offer, consider the entire compensation package holistically.

Evaluate the salary, benefits, growth opportunities, work-life balance, company culture, and long-term career prospects.

Look for alignment with your personal and professional goals. Assess the value of the overall package rather than fixating solely on salary.

Conclusion

Handling salary negotiations and benefits discussions requires preparation, confidence, and professionalism.

By researching market value, knowing your worth, deferring salary discussions, highlighting your value proposition, expressing flexibility, articulating your expectations, actively listening, asking questions, negotiating with professionalism, and evaluating the entire package, you can navigate these conversations successfully.

Remember, maintaining open communication and aiming for a win-win outcome can lead to a mutually beneficial agreement that meets both your financial expectations and your long-term career goals.

Following Up After the Interview

The job interview doesn't end when you walk out of the door.

Following up after the interview is a crucial step in the hiring process. It allows you to express gratitude, reiterate your interest in the position, and keep yourself at the forefront of the interviewer's mind.

In this chapter, we will explore effective strategies for following up after the interview.

Sending a Thank-You Email

Within 24 hours of the interview, send a personalized thank-you email to each interviewer.

Express your appreciation for their time, the opportunity to learn more about the company, and the chance to discuss your qualifications. Highlight specific aspects of the interview that resonated with you, such as a particular discussion or insight.

Keep the email concise, professional, and genuine.

Reaffirming Your Interest

Use the follow-up communication to reiterate your enthusiasm for the position and the company.

Mention specific reasons why you are excited about the opportunity, such as alignment with the company's values, growth potential, or the chance to contribute to their mission.

This reaffirms your interest and showcases your commitment to the role.

Sharing Additional Information
If during the interview you promised to provide additional information or references, include them in your follow-up email.

This demonstrates your attention to detail and follow-through. Attach any relevant documents, such as a portfolio, writing samples, or certifications, that can further showcase your qualifications.

Addressing Unanswered Questions

If there were any questions or topics that remained unanswered during the interview, take the opportunity to address them in your follow-up communication.

This shows your commitment to thoroughness and ensures that all relevant information is provided to the interviewer.

Personalizing Each Follow-Up

If you interviewed with multiple individuals, tailor each follow-up message to reflect the specific conversation you had with each person.

Reference a specific point discussed, a shared interest, or a notable insight.

Personalizing your follow-up messages demonstrates your attentiveness and helps you stand out among other candidates.

Professional Social Media Connections

Consider connecting with the interviewers on professional networking platforms, such as LinkedIn, if it aligns with your personal strategy.

Personalize your connection request with a brief message expressing your gratitude for the opportunity to interview.

This can help you maintain a professional relationship and stay informed about potential updates.

Patience and Timing

While it is important to follow up promptly, exercise patience and allow the appropriate amount of time for the hiring process to unfold.

Avoid excessive or overly persistent follow-ups that may be seen as pushy. If the interviewer provided a timeline for the next steps, respect it and follow up accordingly if the specified timeframe has passed.

Professional Phone Follow-Up

In some cases, a professional phone call may be appropriate for a follow-up.

Use this method selectively, such as when you have not received a response to your email or when the interviewer expressed a preference for phone communication.

When making the call, be prepared, articulate, and respectful of the interviewer's time.

Gracious Acceptance or Rejection

Once you receive an offer or notification of the outcome, respond promptly and graciously.

If accepting the offer, express your gratitude, reiterate your enthusiasm, and discuss next steps.

If the outcome is not in your favor, respond politely, expressing your appreciation for the opportunity and your interest in future opportunities with the company.

Conclusion

Following up after the interview is a vital step in the job search process.

By sending a thank-you email, reaffirming your interest, sharing additional information, addressing unanswered questions, personalizing each follow-up, connecting professionally on social media, being patient and timely, considering professional phone follow-up, and responding graciously to offers or rejections, you can leave a positive and lasting impression on the interviewer.

Remember, effective follow-up communication demonstrates professionalism, gratitude, and continued interest in the position.

Overcoming Rejection and Learning from Setbacks

Experiencing rejection during the job search process is a common and often disheartening occurrence.

However, it's important to view rejection as an opportunity for growth and learning.

In this chapter, we will explore strategies to overcome rejection, bounce back from setbacks, and turn them into stepping stones toward future success.

Acknowledge and Process Your Emotions

Receiving a rejection can be emotionally challenging. Allow yourself to acknowledge and process your emotions.

It's natural to feel disappointed, frustrated, or even discouraged.

Give yourself time to reflect on these emotions but avoid dwelling on them for too long. Accepting and understanding your feelings will help you move forward.

Seek Feedback and Constructive Criticism

Requesting feedback from the interviewer or hiring manager can provide valuable insights.

While not all companies may be able to provide detailed feedback, it's worth asking. Constructive criticism can help you identify areas for improvement and refine your approach for future opportunities.

Embrace feedback as an opportunity for growth rather than taking it personally.

Review and Reflect on the Interview

Take the time to review your interview performance objectively. Consider both your strengths and areas where you can enhance your skills or responses.

Reflect on any gaps in your knowledge or experience that may have contributed to the rejection. Use this self-assessment to create a plan for personal and professional development.

Maintain a Positive Mindset

Rejection can be demoralizing, but it's essential to maintain a positive mindset.

Remind yourself that rejection is a part of the job search process for everyone. Focus on your strengths, achievements, and the value you bring to potential employers.

Cultivate a resilient attitude that allows you to bounce back and stay motivated.

Reframe Rejection as an Opportunity

View rejection as an opportunity for growth and redirection.

Recognize that it may be a sign that the role or company wasn't the best fit for you.

Use the experience to reassess your career goals, refine your job search strategy, and explore new avenues that align with your interests and skills.

Learn from the Experience

Extract lessons from the rejection and learn from the experience. Consider the interview as a learning opportunity to sharpen your interview skills and enhance your preparation. Analyze the questions asked, the aspects that went well, and the areas where you can improve.

Apply these lessons to future interviews and strive for continuous growth.

Strengthen Your Skill Set

Identify areas where you can enhance your skills and knowledge.

Invest in professional development opportunities, such as online courses, workshops, or certifications, to broaden your skill set and make yourself a more competitive candidate.

Strengthening your skills not only increases your chances of success but also boosts your confidence.

Maintain a Support Network

Lean on your support network during times of rejection. Seek guidance, encouragement, and advice from friends, family, mentors, or career coaches.

Surround yourself with individuals who uplift and motivate you, providing a fresh perspective and helping you stay focused on your goals.

Stay Persistent and Resilient

Maintain persistence and resilience in the face of rejection.

Remember that each rejection brings you closer to finding the right opportunity. Stay committed to your job search efforts, continue refining your skills and application materials, and remain open to new possibilities.

A resilient attitude and consistent effort will increase your chances of success.

Conclusion

Overcoming rejection and learning from setbacks is a vital part of the job search journey.

By acknowledging and processing your emotions, seeking feedback, reviewing, and reflecting on interviews, maintaining a positive mindset, reframing rejection as an opportunity, learning from the experience, strengthening your skill set, maintaining a support network, staying persistent, and resilient, you can bounce back stronger and move closer to finding the right job.

Remember, setbacks are temporary, and each rejection brings you one step closer to your ultimate success.

Acing Virtual and Remote Interviews

With the rise of remote work and technological advancements, virtual interviews have become increasingly common.

Acing a virtual or remote interview requires specific strategies and considerations to make a strong impression and effectively communicate your qualifications.

In this chapter, we will explore tips and techniques to excel in virtual and remote interviews.

Test and Optimize Your Technology

Prior to the interview, test your technology setup to ensure a smooth experience.

Check your internet connection, camera, and microphone.

Familiarize yourself with the video conferencing platform being used and troubleshoot any potential issues. Test lighting and sound quality to ensure you come across professionally and clearly.

Create a Professional Background

Choose a clean and clutter-free area for your interview background. Remove any distractions or personal items that may detract from your professionalism.

Consider using a virtual background or setting up a neat and professional backdrop. Pay attention to lighting to ensure your face is well-illuminated.

Dress Professionally

Even though the interview is taking place remotely, dress professionally as you would for an in-person interview.

Your attire should reflect the company culture and the position you are applying for.

Dressing professionally not only demonstrates respect for the opportunity but also helps you feel confident and ready to make a strong impression.

Minimize Distractions

Find a quiet and private space where you won't be interrupted during the interview.

Inform those around you about the interview schedule to minimize disturbances. Close unnecessary applications and silence your mobile phone to avoid distractions.

Creating a focused environment allows you to give your full attention to the interview.

Maintain Eye Contact and Body Language

Maintaining eye contact is essential in virtual interviews. Look directly into the camera to simulate eye contact with the interviewer.

Pay attention to your body language, sitting up straight and maintaining a professional posture. Smile and nod appropriately to convey engagement and attentiveness.

Practice Clear and Concise Communication

Virtual interviews may have slight delays, so it's important to speak clearly and at a moderate pace.

Practice concise and well-structured responses to questions. Take brief pauses before answering to ensure you fully understand the question and gather your thoughts.

Be mindful of any audio lag and allow the interviewer to finish speaking before responding.

Utilize Visual Aids and Digital Materials

Take advantage of the virtual format by utilizing visual aids and digital materials.

Prepare a digital portfolio or presentation to showcase your work or accomplishments. Share your screen to demonstrate your skills or walk the interviewer through relevant documents.

Ensure that your materials are easily accessible and well-organized.

Engage with Active Listening

Engage in active listening during the virtual interview. Demonstrate your attentiveness and understanding by nodding and using verbal cues.

Paraphrase or restate questions to confirm your understanding before providing your response. Active listening shows your genuine interest and allows for effective communication.

Be Prepared for Technical Issues

Despite careful preparation, technical issues can still occur during virtual interviews.

Have a backup plan in case of unexpected disruptions, such as a dropped internet connection or audio problems.

Provide the interviewer with an alternative contact method, such as a phone number, to reconnect if necessary. Stay calm and adaptable if technical challenges arise.

Follow-Up with a Thank-You Email

Just like with in-person interviews, follow up with a thank-you email after the virtual interview.

Express your appreciation for the opportunity, reiterate your interest in the position, and briefly summarize key points from the conversation.

Use this opportunity to reaffirm your fit for the role and showcase your professionalism.

Conclusion

Acing virtual and remote interviews requires adapting to the unique challenges and opportunities of the digital format.

By testing your technology, creating a professional background, dressing professionally, minimizing distractions, maintaining eye contact and body language, practicing clear communication, utilizing visual aids, engaging with active listening, being prepared for technical issues, and following up with a thank-you email, you can navigate virtual interviews with confidence and leave a lasting impression on the interviewer.

Embrace the flexibility of remote interviews and use them to showcase your skills and qualifications effectively.

Special Tips for Technical and Industry-Specific Interviews

Technical and industry-specific interviews require a unique set of skills and knowledge beyond general interview preparation.

These interviews often assess your technical expertise, problem-solving abilities, and industry-specific knowledge.

In this chapter, we will explore special tips and strategies to excel in technical and industry-specific interviews.

Review Technical Concepts and Skills

For technical interviews, it's crucial to review and refresh your knowledge of technical concepts and skills relevant to the position.

Identify the key technical areas that are likely to be assessed and dedicate time to study and practice them.

Review coding languages, algorithms, data structures, or any other technical topics specific to your field.

Solve Practice Problems and Complete Projects

Engage in practice problems and projects that simulate real-world scenarios you may encounter in the industry-specific interview.

Solve coding challenges, work on case studies, or complete projects that demonstrate your technical abilities.

Practice not only enhances your skills but also builds your confidence in applying them effectively.

Stay Updated with Industry Trends

Stay informed about the latest trends, advancements, and challenges in your industry.

Research industry publications, news articles, blogs, and forums to gain insights into current industry discussions.

Familiarize yourself with recent developments, emerging technologies, and any significant changes that may impact the industry.

Understand the Company's Technology Stack

If possible, gather information about the specific technologies and tools used by the company.

Research their technology stack and become familiar with the platforms, frameworks, and software they employ.

Understanding the company's technology stack demonstrates your interest and preparedness for the role.

Prepare Industry-Specific Examples

In industry-specific interviews, be prepared to provide specific examples of your experience and achievements in that particular industry.

Highlight projects or initiatives you have worked on that align with the company's industry.

Clearly articulate your contributions and the results you achieved.

Demonstrate Problem-Solving Skills

Technical and industry-specific interviews often assess your problem-solving abilities.

Be prepared to tackle technical challenges, algorithms, or case studies presented to you during the interview.

Explain your thought process, break down complex problems, and demonstrate logical reasoning in your approach.

Communicate Effectively with Non-Technical Interviewers

In some cases, you may face non-technical interviewers who assess your suitability for the role from a broader perspective.

It's important to communicate your technical knowledge in a clear and concise manner without overwhelming them with jargon.

Tailor your explanations to suit the interviewer's level of understanding.

Showcase Relevant Projects and Work Samples

Prepare a portfolio of relevant projects and work samples to showcase your technical expertise.

Provide documentation, code samples, or demonstrations of projects that highlight your problem-solving skills, technical proficiency, and industry-specific knowledge.

These tangible examples can reinforce your qualifications during the interview.

Be Prepared for Technical Tests or Assessments

Some technical interviews may include practical tests or assessments to evaluate your skills in real-time.

Familiarize yourself with the format and requirements of these assessments, and practice solving similar problems under time constraints. Brush up on any specific tools or frameworks that may be utilized.

Seek Industry-Specific Interview Resources and Communities

Take advantage of industry-specific interview resources, forums, or communities where professionals share their interview experiences and tips.

Engaging with these resources can provide valuable insights and help you understand common interview practices and expectations within your industry.

Conclusion

Preparing for technical and industry-specific interviews requires focused efforts to enhance your technical skills, industry knowledge, and problem-solving abilities.

By reviewing technical concepts, solving practice problems, staying updated with industry trends, understanding the company's technology stack, preparing relevant examples, demonstrating effective problem-solving skills, communicating with non-technical interviewers, showcasing relevant projects, being prepared for technical tests, and seeking industry-specific resources, you can confidently navigate these specialized interviews and position yourself as a strong candidate within your field.

Ethical and Professional Conduct in Interviews

Maintaining ethical and professional conduct throughout the interview process is essential for building a positive reputation, fostering trust, and increasing your chances of success.

In this chapter, we will explore the importance of ethical behavior and professionalism in interviews and provide guidelines to uphold these principles.

From honesty and integrity, to respect and confidentiality.

Honesty and Integrity

The foundation of ethical conduct is honesty and integrity.

Be truthful and transparent in all aspects of the interview process. Provide accurate information about your qualifications, experiences, and achievements. Avoid embellishing or misrepresenting your skills or credentials.

Upholding honesty and integrity builds trust and credibility with interviewers.

Respect and Professionalism

Demonstrate respect and professionalism towards everyone you interact with during the interview process, including interviewers, HR personnel, and other candidates.

Treat everyone with courtesy, regardless of their position or role. Be punctual, dress appropriately, and maintain a professional demeanor throughout the entire process.

Confidentiality and Non-Disclosure

Respect the confidentiality of any sensitive information discussed during the interview.

Interviewers may share details about their company's strategies, projects, or proprietary information.

Do not disclose or discuss this information outside the interview context, as it reflects your ability to handle confidential matters responsibly.

Proper Use of Company Resources

During the interview, you may be given access to company resources such as documents, presentations, or software for assessment purposes.

Use these resources solely for their intended purposes and refrain from unauthorized copying, downloading, or sharing of such materials.

Respect the company's intellectual property rights.

Equal Opportunity and Non-Discrimination

Adhere to principles of equal opportunity and non-discrimination throughout the interview process.

Treat all candidates fairly and respectfully, regardless of their background, race, gender, age, religion, or any other protected characteristic.

Focus on assessing qualifications and merit when evaluating candidates.

Proper Etiquette in Communication

Maintain proper etiquette in all forms of communication during the interview process.

Be polite, professional, and concise in your emails, phone calls, or any other interactions. Use appropriate language and avoid engaging in disrespectful or offensive behavior.

Respond promptly to communication and express gratitude for the opportunity.

Avoiding Conflicts of Interest

Be mindful of potential conflicts of interest that may arise during the interview process.

If you have any existing personal or professional relationships with individuals involved in the hiring process, disclose them appropriately.

Avoid situations that may compromise the fairness and impartiality of the selection process.

Preparedness and Active Engagement

Demonstrate preparedness and active engagement during interviews.

Conduct thorough research about the company, position, and industry beforehand. Ask thoughtful and relevant questions that demonstrate your interest and understanding.

Show enthusiasm, listen attentively, and actively participate in the conversation.

Adhering to the Company's Code of Conduct

Familiarize yourself with the company's code of conduct and ethical guidelines.

Respect and align your behavior with these standards during the interview process.

Companies appreciate candidates who demonstrate an understanding of their values and exhibit behaviors consistent with their organizational culture.

Follow-Up and Appreciation

After the interview, express appreciation for the opportunity by sending a thank-you note or email to the interviewers.

Show gratitude for their time, consideration, and insights shared during the interview.

This gesture reflects your professionalism and respect for the interviewers' investment in the process.

Conclusion

Ethical and professional conduct in interviews not only reflects your character but also influences how you are perceived by potential employers.

By maintaining honesty, integrity, respect, confidentiality, non-discrimination, proper use of resources, and adherence to etiquette, you can build a reputation as a trustworthy and professional candidate.

Upholding these principles throughout the interview process will positively contribute to your career advancement.

Excelling in Panel and Group Interviews

Panel and group interviews are common selection methods used by organizations to assess candidates' abilities to work well in team settings and handle group dynamics.

Excelling in these types of interviews requires specific strategies to navigate the dynamics and stand out among multiple interviewers or candidates.

In this chapter, we will explore tips and techniques to excel in panel and group interviews.

Research the Panel Members

Before the interview, research the backgrounds and roles of the panel members.

Understanding their positions within the organization can help you tailor your responses and engage with them more effectively.

This knowledge also allows you to address specific concerns or interests they may have.

Maintain Eye Contact with All Panel Members

During the interview, make an effort to maintain eye contact with each panel member.

When answering a question, direct your response to the person who asked it initially but periodically shift your gaze to include others.

This inclusive approach demonstrates your ability to engage with multiple stakeholders.

Address Each Panel Member by Name

Whenever possible, address panel members by their names when responding to questions or engaging in discussion.

This personal touch helps establish a connection and shows that you have done your research.

However, use names sparingly to avoid sounding forced or unnatural.

Balance Individual and Group Engagement

In group interviews where multiple candidates are present, strike a balance between individual and group engagement. Contribute actively to the group discussions, listening attentively to others' perspectives, and building upon their ideas.

Additionally, seize opportunities to showcase your individual strengths and experiences when appropriate.

Adapt to Different Interviewer Styles

Panel interviews often involve interviewers with varying styles and personalities.

Adapt to each interviewer's style by observing their communication preferences and adjusting your responses accordingly. Some may prefer concise answers, while others may appreciate more detailed explanations.

Flexibility in your communication style demonstrates your ability to adapt to different team dynamics.

Demonstrate Collaboration and Teamwork

Emphasize your ability to collaborate and work effectively in a team environment.

When engaging with other candidates, listen actively, show respect, and offer support or constructive feedback when appropriate.

Highlight your past experiences of successful teamwork and describe how you contribute to a positive group dynamic.

Be a Leader in Group Activities

If the interview includes group activities or exercises, take the initiative to lead or facilitate the discussion when appropriate.

Display leadership qualities such as effective communication, problem-solving, and decision-making.

Encourage and involve others, ensuring that the group works together towards a common goal.

Stay Calm and Manage Nervousness

Panel interviews can be overwhelming due to the number of interviewers and the competitive nature of the process.

Practice relaxation techniques to manage nervousness, such as deep breathing or positive visualization.

Maintain a confident and composed demeanor, showcasing your ability to handle pressure in a team setting.

Follow-Up with Individual Thank-You Notes

After the panel interview, send individual thank-you notes to each panel member.

Personalize your messages, highlighting specific points of the discussion or aspects you appreciated.

This individualized approach demonstrates your attention to detail and genuine appreciation for each interviewer's contributions.

Review and Reflect on the Experience

After the panel interview, take time to review and reflect on the experience. Assess your performance, identifying areas where you excelled and areas for improvement.

Consider what you learned from the group dynamics and how you can apply those insights to future team-oriented situations.

Conclusion

Excelling in panel and group interviews requires adaptability, teamwork, and strong communication skills.

By researching the panel members, maintaining eye contact, addressing individuals by name, balancing individual and group engagement, demonstrating collaboration, staying calm, and following up with individual thank-you notes, you can navigate these interviews successfully and showcase your ability to thrive in team environments.

Preparing for Second and Final Rounds

Making it to the second or final round of interviews is a significant accomplishment that brings you one step closer to securing the job offer.

These rounds often involve more in-depth assessments and may include additional interviewers or higher-level decision makers.

In this chapter, we will explore strategies to effectively prepare for second and final rounds to increase your chances of success.

Review Previous Interviews

Before the second or final round, thoroughly review your performance and feedback from previous interviews. Identify areas where you excelled and areas that could be improved.

Use this feedback as a foundation for your preparation and focus on strengthening any weaknesses.

Research the Interviewers

Gain insights into the background and roles of the interviewers you will be meeting in the second or final round.

Research their professional profiles, contributions to the company, and any recent achievements or publications.

Understanding their perspectives and areas of expertise can help you tailor your responses and connect with them effectively.

Expand Your Knowledge of the Company

Deepen your understanding of the company and its industry as you progress to the later interview stages. Research recent news, industry trends, and the company's strategic direction.

Familiarize yourself with their competitors, challenges, and opportunities.

This knowledge will enable you to demonstrate a genuine interest and alignment with the organization.

Prepare for Advanced Technical or Scenario-Based Questions

Second or final rounds may involve more advanced technical questions or scenario-based assessments.

Anticipate these types of questions based on the position and industry and prepare accordingly.

Review technical concepts, practice problem-solving, and be ready to apply your knowledge to real-world situations.

Reflect on Your Fit with the Company Culture

Consider your fit with the company culture and values as you advance to later interview stages.

Reflect on your own values and how they align with the organization's mission and culture.

Prepare examples that demonstrate your compatibility with their values and emphasize your ability to contribute positively to their work environment.

Prepare Success Stories and Achievements

Identify your key success stories and achievements that showcase your skills, expertise, and ability to deliver results.

Prepare concise and compelling narratives that highlight the challenges you faced, the actions you took, and the outcomes you achieved.

These stories will serve as strong evidence of your capabilities during the final rounds.

Practice Answering Tough Questions

Expect more challenging questions in the second or final rounds.

Practice responding to questions that assess your problem-solving abilities, decision-making skills, and leadership potential.

Anticipate behavioral questions that probe into specific situations and prepare well-structured and concise responses that showcase your competencies.

Seek Feedback and Guidance

If possible, seek feedback from mentors, career advisors, or individuals familiar with the company or industry.

Their insights can help you identify blind spots, refine your interview strategies, and gain a fresh perspective.

Additionally, consider seeking guidance on negotiating salary or discussing benefits, as these topics may arise in later rounds.

Review and Revisit Company Research

Refresh your knowledge about the company, its mission, and recent developments.

Revisit the company's website, annual reports, press releases, and social media profiles. Pay attention to any updates or changes since your previous interviews.

Being up to date demonstrates your ongoing interest and commitment.

Mock Interviews and Role-Playing

Engage in mock interviews or role-playing sessions with a trusted friend, mentor, or professional contact.

Simulate the interview scenario and practice answering questions, handling challenging situations, and conveying your qualifications confidently.

Receive constructive feedback and work on improving your overall performance.

Confidence and Self-Assurance

Approach the second or final round with confidence and self-assurance.

Build on your past successes, acknowledge your strengths, and believe in your ability to excel in the interview.

Project a positive and professional demeanor throughout the process, showcasing your readiness for the role and your commitment to making a meaningful impact.

Conclusion

Preparing for second and final rounds requires focused effort and a deeper level of research and practice.

By reviewing previous interviews, researching the interviewers and the company, expanding your knowledge, preparing success stories, practicing tough questions, seeking feedback, and approaching the process with confidence, you can position yourself as the top candidate and increase your chances of securing the job offer.

Resources for Continuous Interview Improvement

Interviewing is a skill that can be continuously honed and improved.

To stay ahead in the job market and maximize your interview performance, it's essential to leverage available resources.

In this chapter, we will explore various resources that can aid in your continuous interview improvement journey.

Interview Preparation Websites

Numerous websites offer valuable resources for interview preparation. These platforms provide tips, sample interview questions, and guidance on various aspects of the interview process.

Explore reputable websites such as Glassdoor, Indeed, Monster, and LinkedIn Learning to access their interview-specific content.

Online Courses and Webinars

Participating in online courses and webinars dedicated to interview preparation can provide structured learning and expert guidance.

Platforms like Udemy, Coursera, and LinkedIn Learning offer courses on various interview-related topics, including behavioral interviews, technical interviews, and communication skills.

Take advantage of these resources to enhance your knowledge and skills.

Mock Interview Services

Engaging in mock interviews with professional services or career coaches can be immensely beneficial. These services simulate real interview scenarios and provide personalized feedback on your performance.

They help you identify strengths, weaknesses, and areas for improvement. Look for reputable mock interview services or seek guidance from career development centers.

Professional Networking

Tap into your professional network for interview preparation support.

Reach out to colleagues, mentors, or alumni who have experience in your field or have recently gone through interviews.

They can provide valuable insights, share their interview experiences, and offer tips on how to excel in specific industries or companies.

Industry-Specific Forums and Communities

Joining online forums and communities focused on your industry or field can provide valuable interview-related information. Websites like Reddit, Quora, and industry-specific forums host discussions where professionals share their interview experiences, offer tips, and answer questions.

Actively participate in these communities to learn from others and stay updated on industry-specific interview practices.

Professional Development Workshops

Attend professional development workshops or seminars that cover interview techniques and best practices. These events are often organized by industry associations, career centers, or professional development organizations.

Participating in these workshops can provide you with practical insights, networking opportunities, and the chance to learn from industry experts.

LinkedIn Groups and Content

Utilize LinkedIn as a platform for interview preparation.

Join industry-specific LinkedIn groups and engage in discussions related to interview strategies and experiences.

Follow thought leaders and experts who share valuable content on interview tips and techniques. LinkedIn can serve as a valuable source of information and networking opportunities.

Career Coaches and Mentors

Consider working with a career coach or mentor who specializes in interview preparation.

These professionals can provide personalized guidance, conduct mock interviews, and offer tailored strategies to enhance your interview performance.

They can also assist in identifying your unique strengths and positioning them effectively during interviews.

Reflect and Learn from Past Interviews

One of the most valuable resources for continuous interview improvement is your own experiences.

Reflect on your past interviews, identify areas for improvement, and learn from your successes and challenges. Consider keeping a journal to document your interview experiences and note key lessons learned for future reference.

Conclusion

Continuous improvement in interview skills is vital for career advancement.

By utilizing resources such as interview preparation websites, books, online courses, mock interview services, networking, industry-specific forums, professional workshops, LinkedIn groups, career coaches, and personal reflection, you can enhance your interview performance and increase your chances of securing desired job opportunities.

Embrace a growth mindset and commit to lifelong learning to continually refine your interviewing skills.

Conclusion: Launching Your Career with Confidence

Congratulations!

You have now equipped yourself with the knowledge, strategies, and skills necessary to navigate the job interview process successfully.

Throughout this book, we have covered a wide range of topics to help you prepare for and excel in interviews.

Now, it's time to summarize your journey and prepare to launch your career with confidence.

Reflect on Your Progress

Take a moment to reflect on how far you have come in your interview preparation journey.

Acknowledge the effort you have invested in researching, practicing, and developing your interview skills.

Recognize your growth and the valuable lessons you have learned throughout the process.

Embrace a Positive Mindset

As you embark on your career, it's essential to embrace a positive mindset. Believe in yourself and your abilities.

Trust that your preparation has equipped you to handle any interview challenge that comes your way.

Cultivate confidence in your skills, knowledge, and potential contributions to future employers.

Apply Your Learnings

The knowledge and skills you have acquired from this book are not meant to stay theoretical.

Put them into practice during your interviews. Apply the strategies, techniques, and advice in real-life situations.

Adapt and refine your approach based on the feedback and experiences you encounter.

Leverage Your Network

Remember the importance of your professional network.

Tap into it for support, guidance, and potential opportunities.

Stay connected with colleagues, mentors, and industry contacts who can provide insights, recommendations, and valuable information about job openings.

Continue Learning and Growing

Interviewing is an ongoing process. As you launch your career, commit to continuous learning and growth.

Seek opportunities to enhance your skills, knowledge, and professional development.

Stay informed about industry trends, technologies, and best practices to remain competitive in your field.

Learn from Setbacks

Setbacks and rejections are part of the job search process.

Instead of being discouraged, view them as learning opportunities.

Reflect on each interview experience, identify areas for improvement, and implement changes accordingly.

Use setbacks as motivation to refine your approach and become a stronger candidate.

Stay Persistent and Resilient

Launching a successful career requires persistence and resilience. Don't let setbacks or rejections deter you from pursuing your goals.

Stay focused, maintain a positive attitude, and keep moving forward.

Remember that each interview is a chance to learn and grow, bringing you closer to finding the right opportunity.

Celebrate Your Achievements

Throughout this journey, celebrate your achievements, both big and small.

Acknowledge your progress, the milestones you have reached, and the valuable skills you have developed.

Recognize your resilience, determination, and commitment to self-improvement.

Seek Feedback and Evolve

As you begin your career, actively seek feedback from employers, colleagues, and mentors.

Embrace constructive criticism as an opportunity for growth. Use the feedback to refine your interviewing skills and make adjustments as needed.

Continually evolving and adapting will help you succeed in the ever-changing job market.

Trust the Process

Lastly, trust the process. The interview process can be challenging, but with the right preparation, mindset, and perseverance, you can achieve your career goals.

Have faith in your abilities and trust that the right opportunity will come along at the right time.

Conclusion

Launching your career with confidence requires thorough preparation, self-reflection, and a positive mindset.

By applying the knowledge and strategies shared in this book, leveraging your network, embracing continuous learning, staying persistent, and seeking feedback, you are well on your way to securing the job of your dreams.

Remember, your journey doesn't end here; it's only the beginning of an exciting and fulfilling professional adventure. Good luck!

Summary

In this final chapter, we will provide a concise summary of the key points and actionable steps discussed throughout this book.

This summary will serve as a handy reference guide to help you navigate the job interview process effectively.

Remember, interview success is not just about ticking off a checklist. It's about authentically showcasing your skills, experiences, and passion for the role. Embrace the process, be yourself, and approach each interview with confidence and enthusiasm.

Good luck in your career endeavors!

The Power of Preparation:

Understand the importance of thorough preparation and how it can significantly impact your interview performance.

Understanding the Interview Process:

Familiarize yourself with the typical stages and formats of interviews to better prepare for each step.

Crafting Your Personal Brand:

Develop a strong personal brand that highlights your unique skills, experiences, and qualities to make a lasting impression on employers.

Researching the Company and Position:

Conduct extensive research on the company and the role you are interviewing for to demonstrate your genuine interest and alignment.

Analyzing the Job Description:

Break down the job description to identify the key skills, qualifications, and responsibilities sought by the employer, enabling you to tailor your responses accordingly.

Unveiling the Hidden Job Market:

Discover strategies to tap into the hidden job market and uncover job opportunities that are not widely advertised.

Polishing Your Resume and Cover Letter:

Craft a compelling resume and cover letter that effectively highlight your qualifications and makes you stand out from other candidates.

Creating an Impressive Portfolio:

Develop a professional portfolio that showcases your work samples, projects, and achievements to demonstrate your capabilities.

Networking and Building Professional Relationships:

Leverage your network to establish valuable connections, gain insights into job opportunities, and receive recommendations and referrals.

Developing a Winning Mindset:

Cultivate a positive mindset, build confidence, and maintain a proactive and motivated attitude throughout the interview process.

Mastering Common Interview Questions:

Familiarize yourself with commonly asked interview questions and practice crafting thoughtful and concise responses.

Nailing Behavioral and Situational Questions:

Prepare compelling stories that demonstrate your abilities to handle challenging situations and showcase relevant skills and experiences.

Handling Challenging Interview Scenarios:

Equip yourself with strategies to tackle challenging interview scenarios such as hypothetical questions, gaps in employment, or conflicts.

Showcasing Your Skills and Experience:

Effectively communicate your skills, experiences, and achievements during the interview to demonstrate your value to potential employers.

Demonstrating Cultural Fit and Teamwork:

Emphasize your ability to fit into the company's culture and work collaboratively with others, highlighting your team-oriented mindset.

Making a Lasting Impression with Body Language:

Understand the importance of body language and non-verbal cues during interviews, and practice conveying confidence and professionalism.

Handling Salary Negotiations and Benefits Discussions:

Learn strategies for negotiating salary and discussing benefits, ensuring you receive fair compensation for your skills and experience.

Following Up After the Interview:

Demonstrate your professionalism by sending personalized thank-you notes and following up with employers after the interview.

Overcoming Rejection and Learning from Setbacks:

Use rejection as an opportunity to learn, grow, and improve your interview skills, and maintain a resilient and positive attitude.

Acing Virtual and Remote Interviews:

Adapt to the virtual interview format and learn how to effectively present yourself in virtual settings, showcasing your communication skills.

Special Tips for Technical and Industry-Specific Interviews:

Prepare for technical and industry-specific interviews by researching the specific requirements, trends, and skills relevant to your field.

Ethical and Professional Conduct in Interviews:

Demonstrate ethical behavior, professionalism, and integrity throughout the interview process, showcasing your character and values.

Excelling in Panel and Group Interviews:

Develop strategies to navigate panel and group interviews, effectively engaging with multiple interviewers or fellow candidates.

Preparing for Second and Final Rounds:

Tailor your preparation for second and final interview rounds, focusing on in-depth company research and reinforcing your suitability for the role.

Resources for Continuous Interview Improvement:

Utilize various resources such as websites, books, courses, networking, workshops, and feedback to continually enhance your interview skills.

Conclusion: Launching Your Career with Confidence:

Reflect on your progress, maintain a positive mindset, apply your learnings, leverage your network, continue learning and growing, and trust the process as you embark on your career journey.

Final Message

Congratulations on completing this comprehensive guide to preparing for job interviews! You have gained valuable insights, strategies, and knowledge to navigate the interview process with confidence. As you embark on your career journey, remember that success is within your reach.

Believe in yourself, trust in your abilities, and stay committed to continuous learning and growth. Embrace every interview as an opportunity to showcase your unique talents and make a positive impression. Even in the face of challenges or setbacks, maintain a resilient mindset and use them as stepping stones towards greater achievements.

Remember, you are not alone on this journey. Reach out to your support network, seek guidance from mentors and career professionals, and share your experiences with others. Embrace collaboration and build meaningful connections throughout your career.

Now it's time to put all your preparation into action. Step into each interview room with confidence, passion, and authenticity. Show the world what you are capable of and let your skills and potential shine.

We wish you the very best as you launch your career with confidence and embark on a fulfilling professional journey. May every interview be an opportunity for growth, success, and the realization of your dreams.

Good luck, and may you achieve all your career aspirations!

www.ingramcontent.com/pod-product-compliance
Lightning Source LLC
Chambersburg PA
CBHW071507220526
45472CB00003B/939